This Ladybird Picture
Book has been specially
planned to illustrate familiar
objects which a child will
enjoy recognizing and
naming. There is just the
right amount of detail in
each one to encourage
comment and conversation
with mother or teacher,
who should talk freely about
the pictures - thus helping
to build up the child's
speech vocabulary. Baby-
talk should always be
avoided.

*The Ladybird Picture Books
are ideally suited for use with
the Ladybird 'Under Five' series—
'Learning with Mother' and its
associated Playbooks.*

A LADYBIRD

Third
Picture
Book

by ETHEL and
HARRY WINGFIELD

Ladybird Books Loughborough

tractor

Talking about the tractor:

Someone has been driving this tractor through the mud!
Look at the marks on the pavement!

0 7214 0281 X

tomatoes

Talking about tomatoes:

One of these tomatoes has been cut up ready to be eaten. You can see the seeds inside.
Do you like tomatoes? These are bright red.

rabbit

Talking about rabbits:

This rabbit lives in a rabbit hutch. It is a pet rabbit.
Some rabbits live in fields and woods.

boat

Talking about the boat:

This boat is floating on the water. It is made of wood.

If you put a piece of wood in the bath water it will float like this boat.

pear

Talking about pears:

Someone has taken a bite out of this pear.
Pears grow on pear trees.

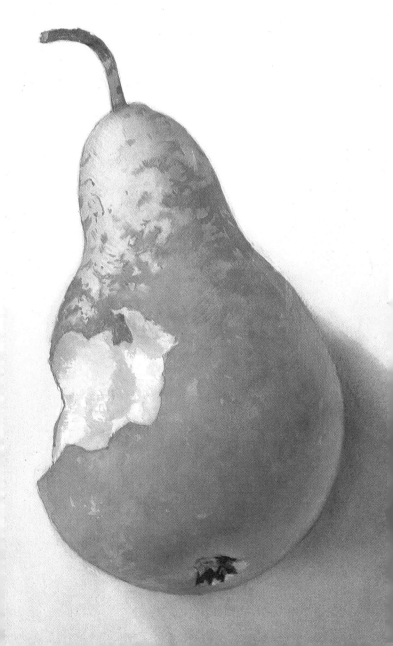

bubbles

Talking about bubbles:

This little girl is blowing large and small bubbles.
Shall we find the largest bubble and the smallest?

cabbage

Talking about cabbages:

This is a cabbage. It is green.
Some people grow cabbages in their gardens.

scissors

Talking about scissors:

Someone has been cutting paper with these scissors. They are so shiny, they look like new ones.

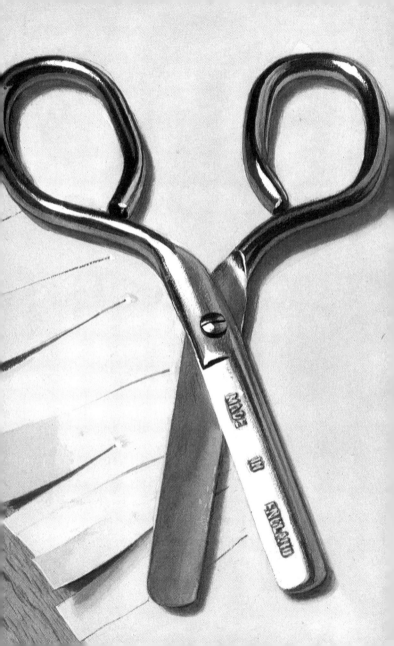

donkey

Talking about donkeys:

This donkey is walking through a field.
Have you ever seen a donkey?
Children can ride on donkeys.

cake

Talking about cake:

What a large slice of cake!
Can you see the sugar on the top, and the cream
and jam inside?

watering can

Talking about the watering-can:

Can you see any water coming out of the
watering-can?
This watering-can is red.

blossom

Talking about blossom:

When a tree has a lot of little flowers on it the flowers are called "blossom".
Can you see some green leaves?

road roller

Talking about road rollers:

Road rollers are very big and heavy.
Have you ever seen a road roller working?

strawberries

Talking about strawberries:

Do you like to eat strawberries?
They can be made into strawberry jam which we
can eat on bread-and-butter.

wellingtons

Talking about wellingtons:

Someone has worn these wellingtons in the rain.
Can you see the drops of rain on them?

slide

Talking about slides:

Do you like to go down a slide?
Can you see the steps?
Shall we count them?

grapes

Talking about grapes:

Here is a picture of some grapes. There are many grapes on this bunch.

Grapes are fruit.

Pears and strawberries are fruit.

wheel-barrow

Talking about wheelbarrows:

If you had a wheelbarrow what would you carry in it?

clock

Talking about the alarm clock:

Here is a special kind of clock, an alarm clock.
Its bell rings to wake you up.

bread

Talking about bread:

This loaf of bread has two slices cut from it.
What would you like to spread on a slice of bread?

shells

Talking about shells:

Shells are the homes of little sea animals. These shells are empty.

You can find shells at the seaside.

milk

Talking about milk:

Do you drink all your milk?
Milk comes from cows.
Cows live on farms.

window

Talking about the window:

Someone has left these windows wide open.

Easter egg

Someone is going to eat this chocolate egg.
The silver paper has been torn.
There is a lovely, yellow ribbon round it.

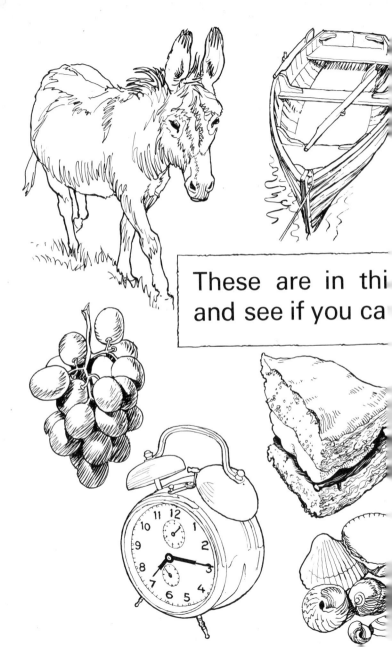

These are in thi
and see if you ca